ANCIENT GREECE
INSIDE OUT

John Malam

Crabtree Publishing Company
www.crabtreebooks.com

Author: John Malam

Editors: Sarah Eason, Kelly Spence, Janine Deschenes, and Kathy Middleton

Editorial director: Kathy Middleton

Design: Paul Myerscough

Cover design: Paul Myerscough

Photo research: Rachel Blount

Proofreader: Wendy Scavuzzo

Production coordinator and Prepress technician: Tammy McGarr

Print coordinator: Margaret Amy Salter

Consultant: John Malam, archaeologist

Written and produced for Crabtree Publishing Company by Calcium Creative

Front Cover
BKGD: The Parthenon, an ancient Greek temple built in Athens in tribute to the goddess Athena
Inset: A kylix, which is a vessel used for drinking wine, from 480 BCE.
Title Page
BKGD: The Agora of Smyrna was the main meeting place for the citizens of the ancient Greek city of Smyrna.
Inset: A re-creation of the Trojan Horse. In Greek mythology, Greek soldiers hid inside a wooden horse and attacked the city of Troy after the Trojans brought it inside their city gates.

Photo Credits:

t=Top, bl=Bottom Left, br=Bottom Right

Alamy: Erin Babnik: p. 17br; Lanmas: p. 21br; Dreamstime: Raphael Heller: p. 12–13; Getty Images: DEA/G. DAGLI ORTI/Contributor: p. 15t; The Getty Museum: Digital image courtesy of the Getty's Open Content Program: p. 25t;

LACMA www.lacma.org: Gift of Varya and Hans Cohn: p. 11br;

Shutterstock: Anastasios71: p. 3, p. 20–21, p. 28–29; Anton_Ivanov: p. 8–9; imagIN.gr photography: p. 26–27 Patryk Kosmider: p. 4–5; Mark and Anna Wilson: p. 18–19; Paul B. Moore: p. 27t; Nadezhda1906: p. 16–17; Sergiy Palamarchuk: p. 10–11; Pecold: p. 6–7; Tatiana Popova: p. 1br, p. 23br; Tolgaildun: p. 1bg, p. 24–25; WitR: p. 14–15; Cristian Zamfir: p. 22–23;

Wikimedia Commons: Collection of Giampietro Campana di Cavelli; 1861: purchased: p. 19t; Carole Raddato from Frankfurt, Germany: p. 9br; Steff: p. 13r.

Map p. 5 by Geoff Ward. Artwork p. 29 by Venetia Dean.

Cover: Shutterstock: Rich Lynch (bg); Louvre Museum, Campana Collection; purchase, 1861 (br).

Library and Archives Canada Cataloguing in Publication

Malam, John, author
       Ancient Greece inside out / John Malam.

(Ancient worlds inside out)
Includes index.
Issued in print and electronic formats.
ISBN 978-0-7787-2876-4 (hardcover).--
ISBN 978-0-7787-2890-0 (softcover).--
ISBN 978-1-4271-1847-9 (HTML)

       1. Greece--Social life and customs--Juvenile literature.
2. Greece--Civilization--To 146 B.C.--Juvenile literature.
3. Greece--Antiquities--Juvenile literature. 4. Material culture--Greece--Juvenile literature. 5. Greece--History--To 146 B.C.--Juvenile literature. I. Title.

DF77.M25 2017   j938   C2016-907259-2
                                                                  C2016-907260-6

Library of Congress Cataloging-in-Publication Data

Names: Malam, John, 1957- author.
Title: Ancient Greece inside out / John Malam.
Description: New York, New York : Crabtree Publishing Company, 2017. | Series: Ancient worlds inside out | Includes index.
Identifiers: LCCN 2017000079 (print) | LCCN 2017005539 (ebook) | ISBN 9780778728764 (reinforced library binding : alkaline paper) | ISBN 9780778728900 (paperback : alkaline paper) | ISBN 9781427118479 (Electronic HTML)
Subjects: LCSH: Greece--Civilization--To 146 B.C.--Juvenile literature. | Greece--Antiquities--Juvenile literature.
Classification: LCC DF77 .M2846 2017 (print) | LCC DF77 (ebook) | DDC 938--dc23
LC record available at https://lccn.loc.gov/2017000079

Crabtree Publishing Company

www.crabtreebooks.com   1-800-387-7650

Printed in Canada/032017/EF20170202

Published in Canada
Crabtree Publishing
616 Welland Ave.
St. Catharines, Ontario
L2M 5V6

Published in the United States
Crabtree Publishing
PMB 59051
350 Fifth Avenue, 59th Floor
New York, New York 10118

Published in the United Kingdom
Crabtree Publishing
Maritime House
Basin Road North, Hove
BN41 1WR

Published in Australia
Crabtree Publishing
3 Charles Street
Coburg North
VIC, 3058

CONTENTS

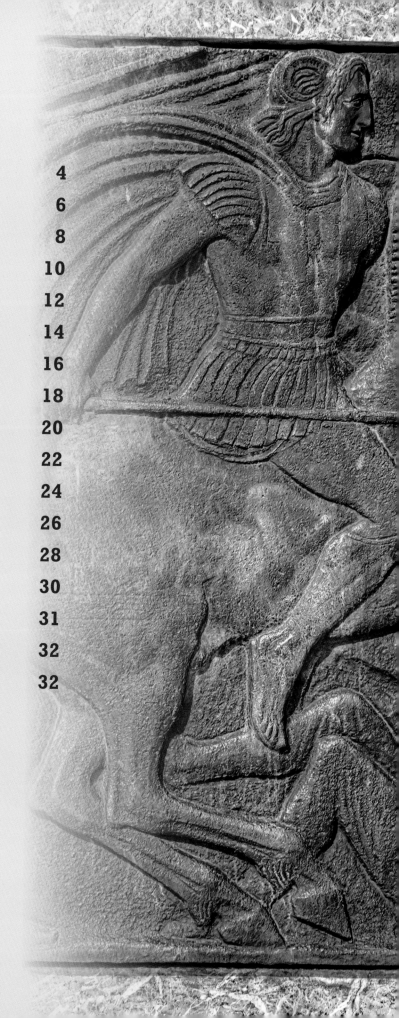

WHO WERE THE ANCIENT GREEKS?

Greece is a country in southeast Europe. It is part of a **peninsula**, which is a piece of land surrounded by water on three sides. The mainland is very rugged, with some mountains reaching all the way down to the sea.

Europe's First Great Civilization

Greece was the place where the first great civilization of Europe flourished. It was at its greatest during the 400s B.C.E., which was about 2,500 years ago. We call the people of this civilization the ancient Greeks. The names "Greek" and "Greece" are modern English names. They come from names first used by the Romans about 2,000 years ago. The Romans called the people of Greece the "Graeci" and the land where they lived "Graecia." The ancient Greeks did not use these names. They called themselves Hellenes, and their land was Hellas.

Masters of the Sea

The sea was very important to the ancient Greeks. Famous Greek **philosopher** Socrates explained its importance in about 410 B.C.E., when he is reported to have said: "We live around a sea like frogs around a pond." With this statement, Socrates explained how the Greek people depended on the sea, hopping on and off ships as easily as frogs jumping in and out of a pond. The ancient Greeks were excellent ship-builders and sailors. Their **merchants** and settlers sailed to faraway lands, their battleships fought against enemy **fleets**, and their fishermen knew where to find the best catches.

What Is an Ancient Civilization?

Large settlements of people formed the basis of the first civilizations. Through practices such as farming and the development of writing systems, government, and social classes, the settlements grew into large cities. These ancient civilizations led to the later development of present-day cities, states, and countries.

More than 2,000 islands belong to Greece. Many were formed by volcanoes. Today, people live on about 200 of the Greek islands.

Key

Ancient Greece around the year 500 B.C.E.

Present-day borders

This map shows the principal **city-states** of ancient Greece.

Macedonia

Albania

Greece

Aegean Sea

Turkey

Thebes ●

Corinth ●   ● Athens

Argos ●   ● Mycenae   ● Ephesus

                                ● Miletus

Sparta ●

Mediterranean Sea

● Knossos

DIGGING UP THE PAST

People first began living in Greece about 40,000 years ago. These early people wandered the land, hunting wild animals and gathering plants. About 8,000 years ago, people started to settle down, or live in the same places for many years. They created villages and began farming the land. Then, around 5,000 years ago, the ancient Greeks found a way to make **bronze**, a type of metal. Bronze was used to make weapons and tools, and helped the ancient Greek civilization grow. This period, around 3000 B.C.E., was called the Bronze Age. During that time, Greece was home to two great civilizations— one on the mainland, and the other on the islands.

Minoans and Mycenaeans

Crete, which is the largest of the Greek islands, was home to the Minoan civilization (3200–1450 B.C.E.). They built grand buildings that archaeologists call "palaces." The finest and largest palace was in the ancient city of Knossos. It had more than 1,000 rooms. The Minoans had their own language and were the first people in Europe to develop a writing system.

The Mycenaeans flourished on the mainland of Greece (1600–1100 B.C.E.). They built small settlements on the hilltops surrounded by strong stone walls. **Archaeologists** call these settlements **citadels**. Several Bronze Age citadels have been excavated, or dug up. The most important citadel uncovered was in Mycenae. Because it was the first to be uncovered, archaeologists named the people of this civilization the Mycenaeans. The Mycenaeans grew in power, and their influence spread from the mainland to the islands. Unlike the Minoans, the Mycenaeans spoke a language similar to present-day Greek. Because of this, they are identified as the first Greeks.

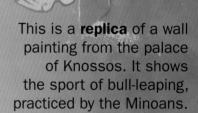

This is a **replica** of a wall painting from the palace of Knossos. It shows the sport of bull-leaping, practiced by the Minoans.

What Are Primary Sources?

Archaeology is the study of how people lived in the past. Archaeologists learn about how and where people lived through the materials they left behind. These materials, called primary sources, were made during a specific period of time, and include **artifacts** and written documents. Examining primary sources gives us clues about how people lived long ago, and how great civilizations **flourished**. Archaeologists **analyze** these objects to **interpret** their meanings.

CITY-STATES AND GOVERNMENT

Ancient Greece was not like the modern country of Greece, which has one capital city called Athens. Instead, in the 400s B.C.E., when ancient Greece was at its greatest, the civilization was a collection of city-states. City-states each had their own laws, armies, and coins, and chose their own leaders. Sometimes city-states went to war against each other, but at other times they joined forces to protect all of ancient Greece from a common enemy.

The City-State of Athens

Athens was the largest and most powerful of the city-states. In the 400s B.C.E., the city-state covered about 1,000 square miles (2,590 sq km) of land. The total population was about 250,000 people. Athens, and other city-states such as Argos and Corinth, was built in two parts. There was a lower city where people lived, worked, and shopped. An upper city, called an **acropolis**, was built on top of a nearby flat-topped hill. In times of danger, the acropolis served as a refuge where people went for safety. It was also where the city's most important temples, sacred statues, and **altars** were built.

Governing the People

Each city-state had its own way of governing its people. There were two forms of government—**oligarchy** and **democracy**. The city-states of Sparta, Corinth, and Thebes were governed as an oligarchy. They were ruled by a few rich and powerful men. For people living in Athens, democracy gave them certain rights, including the right to vote. Although living in a democracy meant that some people had the power to decide who would run the state, many others had little or no say in their government. Only **citizens**, or men aged 18 and above and born in Athens, were allowed to vote. Women and slaves could not vote.

The agora of Athens was the city center and main market area.

Unique to Athens was the practice of banishing, or sending away, a politician from the city-state. It was a way of preventing too much power from falling into one man's hands. Male citizens would gather in the **agora** to cast their votes on who should be banished. Each man would scratch the name of a politician on a small piece of pottery. The man who received the most votes was given ten days to pack and then was forced to leave Athens for ten years. The pieces of broken pottery were called "ostraka." The English word "**ostracize**," which means to banish or cast out, comes from this ancient Greek word. This ostrakon, which dates from 482 B.C.E., bears the name of a politician named Themistocles.

ostrakon

THE FAMILY IN ANCIENT GREECE

A typical family in ancient Greece included a father, mother, and their children, who all lived together in the same house. The father was the head of the family, and he might allow other people to live in the house, such as the children's grandparents, their unmarried or **widowed** aunts, and the family's slaves, if they had any.

Men and Women

Men and women were not treated as equals in ancient Greece. Men were allowed to do many more things than women, such as own property and land, vote in elections, and take part in **politics**. Women could not own or inherit property or land, and could not vote or get involved in politics. Instead, they were expected to stay at home, look after the children, and do everyday housework, such as weaving fabric, making clothes, cooking, and cleaning.

Boys and Girls

The inequality between genders began from birth. To their parents, boys were considered more useful than girls. This was because boys would one day inherit their father's land and property, ensuring it stayed within the family. Girls could also be more expensive for a family. When a girl married, her parents had to give a **dowry** of money, goods, or property to her new husband. They did not need to save up a dowry for a son. Boys went to school and were taught reading, writing, arithmetic, poetry, dancing, athletics, and how to play musical instruments. Girls stayed home and were taught how to cook, weave wool, and make clothes. It prepared them for married life. While girls usually married at about the age of 15, boys married when they were much older—usually when they were men in their 20s or 30s.

History Up Close

Most clothes were made from wool or linen, both of which produced creamy-white fabrics. For that reason, clothes ended up being this natural color. Only the rich could afford colored clothes, dyed red and yellow or purple. Men, women, and children wore simple loose-fitting tunics, which could be long or short. This pottery figure of an ancient Greek woman was made in the 200s B.C.E. She is shown wearing a chiton—a one-piece woolen garment held in place at the shoulders by brooches or pins. It was gathered in at the waist by a belt, and reached down to the ground.

Archaeologists have uncovered the remains of ancient Greek towns. These buildings are carefully preserved so that people can study how and where ancient Greeks once lived.

statue of
a female

FOOD AND FARMING

Most people in ancient Greece farmed the land. The rich soil along the coast was ideal for growing crops. Farther inland toward the mountains, the soil was less fertile, making it more difficult to grow plants. Olives, and grains such as barley and wheat were among the most important crops harvested by the ancient Greeks.

Grains

Grain was so important to the survival of the ancient Greeks that they prayed to their gods for good harvests. Demeter is the Greek goddess of farming and grain. Around 700 B.C.E., the poet Hesiod wrote in his poem *Works and Days*: "Pray to Zeus of the earth and pure Demeter for Demeter's holy grain to ripen heavy…In this way the ears [of grain] may nod towards the earth with thickness…" Prayers alone did not guarantee a healthy crop. Farmers also used tools such as plows to turn the soil, and dug channels for water to **irrigate** the fields. Each year, they also rotated the kinds of crops they planted in their fields. Since different crops need different **nutrients** in the soil, rotating crops meant that nutrients would not be overused year after year.

Olives

Olives, and the oil they produce, were highly prized in ancient Greek society. People believed that the olive tree was a gift from Athena, the **patron** goddess of Athens. The oil in particular had many uses. It was used for cooking and burned in lamps for light. At sports events, winners were crowned with a wreath of olive branches, and awarded large amounts of oil as a prize. Olives were also left as offerings to the gods and to honor the memories of **ancestors**.

Olive trees still cover much of Greece. Some trees are thousands of years old and continue to produce olives that are harvested.

History Up Close

This vase dates from about 520 B.C.E. It is called an *amphora*, which means "to carry on both sides." Amphorae were used to store foods such as grains and oils, and drinks such as wine. The scene painted on the side of this vase shows how olives were harvested by the ancient Greeks. One young boy sits high in the tree and uses a stick to knock down olives, and a boy on the ground gathers them in a basket. Two adults use longer sticks to knock the ripe olives from the branches. The falling olives are shown as black dots.

amphora

Dig Deeper!

Why might the ancient Greeks have used the method shown on the vase to harvest olives? What are some advantages and disadvantages to this process? Explain your reasoning.

THEATER AND PLAYS

Actors, dancers, and singers began performing on stage in Athens about 2,500 years ago. Performances were originally part of a religious festival held each March, when groups of men danced and sang in the city's marketplace. Over time, words were written for the men to speak. These were the first plays.

Serious and Funny Plays

Two styles of plays developed in Athens—**tragedy** and **comedy**. A tragedy was a serious play, often about the **heroes** of Greek **myths**. The play usually had a sad or tragic ending. Sophocles, Euripides, and Aeschylus are the three most famous tragic playwrights. A playwright is a person who writes plays. Many of their plays have been preserved. The opposite of a tragedy was a comedy. In this type of play, actors performed scenes from everyday life, often making fun of politicians. The audience laughed, and found the plot easy to follow. The playwright Aristophanes wrote many comedies.

Stage and Actors

Most ancient Greek cities had an open-air theater. It was often built inside a natural bowl-shaped hollow, or low area, in the landscape, with tiers of seats carved out of the stone. Plays were performed during the day because it was too dark to see at night. Actors, who were all men, performed on a circular platform, similar to a stage in a modern theater. They sang or spoke their lines, and wore bulky, padded costumes, wigs, and shoes with thick soles to look taller. Costume colors indicated the mood of the play. Bright colors were worn in a comedy, and dark colors in a tragedy. These larger-than-life costumes allowed people sitting in the back to easily see the actors.

History Up Close

Actors wore painted masks over their faces, held on with cord. Masks were made from wood, cork, clay, or stiffened cloth, and their features were exaggerated with big eyes and noses, and wide mouths shaped like funnels. Masks made it easier for the audience to figure out if an actor was playing a funny or serious character, a man or a woman, or a young or old person. When the actor spoke, the funneled mouth shape on the mask amplified his voice, which means that it came out loudly so it could be heard by the whole audience. This **terra-cotta** mask dates from 300–200 B.C.E.

theater mask

The ancient Greek theater at Epidaurus could seat 14,000 people, who watched actors perform on the center circle.

Dig Deeper!

Examine the expression on the mask shown above. Do you think it was used in a comedy or tragedy? Why?

GODS AND THEIR TEMPLES

The ancient Greeks worshiped many gods. They imagined them looking like people, but with superhuman powers. The most important gods were a family of 12, who were believed to live at the top of Mount Olympus, the tallest mountain in Greece. They were named the Olympian gods, after their mountain home.

The Gods of Mount Olympus

These are the gods and goddesses often considered to make up the 12 Olympians, but some lists of 12 can be different from this one.

Aphrodite—goddess of love and beauty

Apollo—god of the Sun, truth, music, poetry, dance, and healing

Ares—god of war

Artemis—goddess of hunting

Athena—goddess of war, wisdom, and art

Demeter—goddess of grain and fertility

Dionysus—god of wine and vegetation

Hades—also called Hephaestus; god of fire, volcanoes, blacksmiths, and craftsmen

Hera—queen of the gods, goddess of women and marriage

Hermes—the messenger of the gods; god of travel and business

Poseidon—god of the sea, earthquakes, and horses

Zeus—king of the gods; god of the heavens and weather

Gifts for the Gods

An ancient Greek **proverb** said: "Gifts persuade the gods." People thought that if they gave a gift to a god, their prayer would be answered. Gifts were given to the gods at their **temples**. The easiest gift to give was a prayer, because it was free. If a person wanted to give more, they might leave food, wine, or clothes. The most expensive gift was an animal, such as a sheep, which would be **sacrificed** on the god's altar. Its meat was cooked, and its bones burned. The smoke from the fire rose into the sky, as if carrying it up to the god or goddess.

16

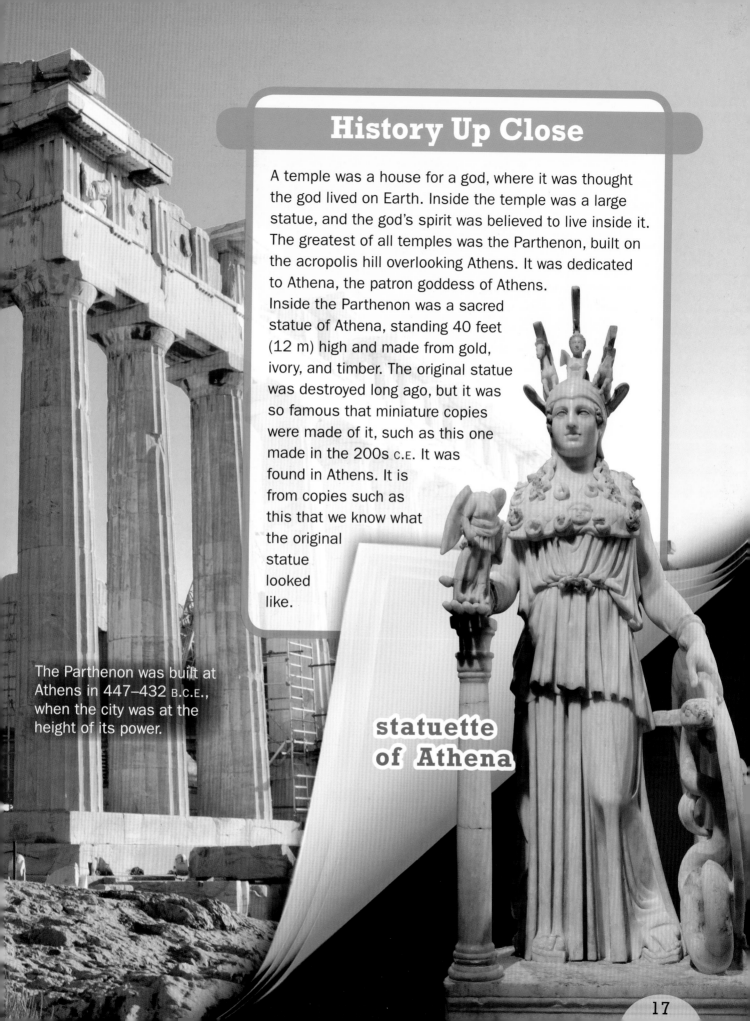

History Up Close

A temple was a house for a god, where it was thought the god lived on Earth. Inside the temple was a large statue, and the god's spirit was believed to live inside it. The greatest of all temples was the Parthenon, built on the acropolis hill overlooking Athens. It was dedicated to Athena, the patron goddess of Athens. Inside the Parthenon was a sacred statue of Athena, standing 40 feet (12 m) high and made from gold, ivory, and timber. The original statue was destroyed long ago, but it was so famous that miniature copies were made of it, such as this one made in the 200s C.E. It was found in Athens. It is from copies such as this that we know what the original statue looked like.

The Parthenon was built at Athens in 447–432 B.C.E., when the city was at the height of its power.

statuette of Athena

SPORTS FESTIVALS

Sports were important to the ancient Greeks, especially to men and boys. They believed that physical exercise helped to develop a boy's character, teaching him about winning and losing, as well as making his body stronger. The ancient Greeks thought that sports and religion were connected, and they held festivals that mixed the two together. The greatest of all sports festivals was the Olympic Games, held in honor of Zeus.

The Gymnasium

Many cities in ancient Greece had a gymnasium where boys and men trained for athletics. The gymnasium was an open-air sports ground. It had a running track, fields for throwing the **discus** and the **javelin**, areas for wrestling and jumping, changing rooms, and bathrooms.

Sports Festivals

At Olympia, in the west of Greece, was a large sports complex, and a major temple dedicated to Zeus, the king of the gods. Once every four years, for five days in August or September, the Olympic Games were held there. It was the greatest sports festival in the ancient world, and men and boys traveled from across Greece to compete in the events. Women were not allowed to take part. Athletes represented the towns they came from. Winning athletes were awarded a crown of olive leaves and a palm frond, or leaf. Winning brought great honor to an athlete and to his town.

These are the ruins of the sports stadium at Epidaurus. Here, foot races were run in a straight line. There were posts at each end of the running track where the athletes turned around and ran back.

History Up Close

This image of a discus thrower appears inside a cup called a *kylix*. It dates from between 510 and 500 B.C.E. The signature of the artist appears inside the circle. The discus was a throwing event in which an athlete threw a heavy stone or bronze disc as far as he could. He made a fast three-quarter turn of his body, then released the discus. It weighed about 5.5 pounds (2.5 kg) and was about 12 inches (30 cm) across. The man who threw the discus the farthest was crowned the winner.

discus thrower

Dig Deeper!

A separate sports festival was held at Olympia for women, known as the Heraean Games. What does a sports competition for women reveal about how they were treated?

THE GREEKS AT WAR

The ancient Greeks fought battles on land and sea. There were times when they fought among themselves, such as when Athens and Sparta fought each other in a war that lasted for 27 years. At other times, Greek city-states joined forces to fight a common enemy, as they did to defeat the Persians.

Army and Navy

Greek armies were mostly made up of foot soldiers. A soldier was called a hoplite, after his large round *hoplon*, or shield. His weapons were a long spear and a sword, and for protection he wore a bronze helmet, armor, and shin guards. On land, hoplites stood in long lines, many rows deep. They held their shields together and marched forward, pointing their spears at the enemy. The plan was to keep in line and push the enemy back, forcing them to retreat from the battlefield. Sea battles were fought with warships called triremes. They were long, narrow ships with bronze battering rams at the front. Rowers moved a trireme quickly through the sea, aiming it at an enemy ship. Its ram smashed through the side of the other ship, letting water in and sinking it.

Greece vs. Persia

In the 300s B.C.E., Macedonia, a kingdom in the north of Greece, became incredibly powerful. When a new king came to the throne there, he decided to conquer the Persian Empire to the east of Greece. His name was Alexander. The Greeks and the Persians were bitter enemies. Between 334 and 323 B.C.E., Alexander's army defeated the Persians. Because he conquered lands and built an empire for Greece, he became known as Alexander the Great.

History Up Close

A **hoplite** soldier wore a metal helmet. It was made from a sheet of bronze, beaten into shape. The helmet protected the soldier's head, neck, and most of his face. It was padded on the inside with leather to make it comfortable to wear. Commanders wore helmets with a tall plume of feathers on the top, running from front to back. This made it easy for their men to see them. Many hoplite helmets have been found. Their bronze metal has turned a greenish color with age, as you can see in this helmet, which was made in the 500s B.C.E. When it was new, the bronze was a shiny yellow.

This wall carving shows Alexander the Great leading his hoplite soldiers into battle. He is shown on his horse Bucephalus, which means "ox-head."

hoplite helmet

WRITING AND PHILOSOPHY

The alphabet was invented by the Phoenicians, an ancient people who lived along the coast of North Africa and the Middle East. When Greek traders saw how useful their alphabet was to keep records, they brought the idea back to Greece.

The Greek Alphabet

The first alphabet in ancient Greece appeared sometime around 750 B.C.E. It was adapted from the Phoenician alphabet. There were 24 letters in the ancient Greek alphabet. The first two were *alpha* (a) and *beta* (b). From these two letters comes the word "alphabet."

Stories and Storytellers

The ancient Greeks had many stories about their mythology and historical events. At first, the stories only existed in spoken form, passed on by word of mouth. Poets and storytellers learned the stories by heart, and recited or sang them in public. Starting in the mid-700s B.C.E., with the adoption of the alphabet, the stories were written down. There were many storytellers in ancient Greece. The greatest of them all was Homer. He wrote two lengthy **epics**—*The Iliad* and *The Odyssey*—about a long war against the city of Troy.

Great Thinkers

Socrates, Plato, and Aristotle were three famous Greek philosophers. These men studied the world around them, trying to make sense of it using **reason**. In 335 B.C.E., Aristotle founded the Lyceum, an Athenian school of philosophy. Students studied philosophy during the morning. **Rhetoric**, the skill of speaking persuasively to influence others, was studied during the afternoon.

Archaeologists have discovered the ruins of an ancient city at Hisarlik, Turkey, that fits Homer's description of Troy.

History Up Close

In *The Odyssey*, Homer writes about how the Greeks fought the **Trojans**, but could not break through the city walls of Troy. At last, the Greeks thought of a trick. They built a giant wooden horse and soldiers hid inside it. The Trojans found the horse and, thinking it was a gift, dragged it into the city. That night, the soldiers climbed out of the horse and opened the city gates for the Greek army to enter. Once inside, the Greek army destroyed the city of Troy. This replica of the Trojan horse stands near Hisarlik, Turkey.

Trojan horse

CRAFTS AND TRADE

There were many different crafts in ancient Greece. Most towns had a workshop district set far away from where people lived, where craftsmen worked. Some districts specialized in a particular craft, such as making pottery, casting metal, or carving stone.

From Rough Stone to Smooth Statue

Statues of gods, athletes, politicians, and animals stood in temples, town squares, and private buildings. The finest statues were carved from smooth white **marble**, which came from Mount Pentelicus, near Athens. To make a marble statue, a sculptor started with a block of rough stone. He chipped away with tools such as **chisels** and **punches**, to make the rough shape of the statue. Then he used finer chisels to smooth the surface. After that, he polished the statue with a sandy powder, removing all traces of tool marks and leaving the surface silky smooth. Last of all, the statue was painted in bright colors, to make it seem lifelike. As we look at ancient Greek statues today, all we see is the natural color of the stone—the paint wore off long ago.

The Marketplace

Towns had an open space known as the agora. It served as a marketplace and social center, where farmers, fishermen, merchants, and craftspeople brought their goods to sell. People paid for goods with silver or gold coins. Each city had its own coins, and traders would only accept coins from their city—they did not accept foreign coins from other cities. Traders also sold goods that were brought in from outside Greece, such as papyrus from Egypt.

History Up Close

Around 500 B.C.E., Greek coins such as the one shown to the right, called a *tetradrachm*, came into use. The goddess Athena appeared on one side. An owl and an olive branch, symbols of the goddess, were featured on the other. The inscription means "of the Athenians." This coin was made around 460–455 B.C.E. Over time, Athenian coins became widely used. This coin was discovered in Hauran, Jordan. As Jordan is a long distance from ancient Greece, this coin shows how far Athenian currency traveled.

tetradrachm

Around the edges of some ancient Greek agoras were shaded areas where traders set up their stalls, and where people could shelter from the heat of the Sun.

PAST TO PRESENT

In 146 B.C.E., Greece became a Roman province. It was ruled over from Italy by the Romans. The Romans admired the culture of Greece and learned from its people. Over time, the Romans passed parts of the Grecian culture on to the people who came after them, and so on, until the present day.

Legacy of Ancient Greece

Many ideas, practices, and objects trace their origins back to ancient Greece. For example, the ancient Greeks have given us the system of democracy, used all over the world. They were also the first to use **trial by jury**, which is the cornerstone of the legal system in many countries today. The English language contains many words from the ancient Greeks. Examples include: antique, geography, book, telephone, and microscope. When people watch a comic or tragic play, the Olympic Games, or a marathon race, they have the ancient Greeks to thank for it.

Preserving Ancient Greece

In the 1700s, wealthy Europeans collected ancient Greek statues and pottery vases. It was fashionable for rich people to decorate their homes with objects from the ancient world. Many of these precious objects are now in museums, where they can be enjoyed by everyone. In the 1800s, the first archaeological excavations took place in Greece. At that time, the aim was to discover the history of the people of ancient Greece. Today, tourists visit the ancient sites of Greece. They might sit in a theater where a comedy or tragedy was once performed, or explore a temple that has stood for 2,500 years.

Restoring the Parthenon

The Parthenon was a beautiful temple built in Athens in the 440s B.C.E. It remained in good condition until 1687, when it was damaged in an explosion. After that, its ruins were scavenged for building stone, and collectors took its marble sculptures away. Today, the Parthenon is rising from the ruins. A project to restore the building began in the 1980s. Old stones have been lifted back into place, and new ones have been carved to fill the gaps. A replica of the original **frieze** has been fitted around the top of the building, and a new museum has been built.

The theater Odeon of Herodes Atticus was built in Athens in the Greek style by the Romans in 161 C.E. It is still used for performances today.

Elgin Marbles

History Up Close

Running around the top of the Parthenon temple was a marble frieze that is known as the Elgin Marbles. It shows a procession, held in Athens every year in honor of Athena, the city's patron goddess. The frieze was carved in the 440s B.C.E., under the direction of the sculptor Phidias. In 1801, a British **diplomat** was given permission to remove the frieze. The sculptures were shipped to England, where they were bought by the British Museum and put on display. Today, the Greek government wants to see the frieze returned to Athens, where it would be placed in a special museum.

MEASURING TIME

The ancient Greeks measured time using a device called a *clepsydra*, which means "water thief." A clepsydra used the controlled flow of water to measure time. A container was filled with water, which then slowly leaked through a small hole in the bottom of the container. Marks on the container showed how much time had passed based on the water flow.

Timing Speeches

The Greek design was an improvement from earlier water clocks used by other civilizations, such as the Egyptians. The ancient Greeks used the clepsydra to measure the length of politicians' speeches. Texts reveal that people requested to stop the flow of water if there was an interruption. Politicians paid attention to the water level to know when to wrap up their speeches when their time ran out.

This clepsydra, made sometime between 500 and 401 B.C.E., was found in the agora of Athens. It would have been placed on top of another vessel. When the clepsydra was filled with water, it dripped through the hole in the bottom into the vessel beneath.

Activity:
Make a Water Clock

Measure time like ancient Greek politicians!

You Will Need:

- Clear, clean 2-liter plastic bottle with a cap that seals tight
- Utility knife
- Marker
- Thumbtack
- Jug of water
- Stopwatch or a cell phone with a timer
- A friend

Instructions

1. Have an adult use the utility knife to cut the bottle in half.
2. Have an adult carefully make a small hole in the cap with a thumbtack. The water will drip through this hole from the top into the bottle. Make sure the cap is sealed tight.
3. Flip the top of the bottle upside-down and set it inside the bottom piece of the cut bottle. It should be a snug fit.
4. Carefully pour water into the upside-down portion. Have a friend start the timer as soon as you start pouring.
5. As each minute passes, mark the water level on the bottom piece. Keep recording until all the water has poured into the bottom bottle.

The Challenge

Pour the water out of the botom bottle. Repeat the process again. How accurate is your water clock? With a friend, take turns making short speeches about something this book has taught you about the ancient Greeks. How is your clepsydra a useful tool?

step 5

GLOSSARY

Note: Some bold-faced words are defined where they appear in the text.

acropolis A hill at the heart of a Greek town or city where the most important temples were built

agora An open space in a town which served as a marketplace and as a social center

altars Flat-topped blocks used for offerings to a god

analyze To examine

ancestors People from who others are descended

archaeologists People who study the past by the materials people left behind

artifacts Objects that help us learn more about the way people lived long ago

bronze A yellowish hard metal made by mixing copper with tin

chisels Metal tools with blades that are used to chip away material

citadels Fortified, or strengthened, places

citizens People with full rights in a city and its state

city-states Self-governing cities and the lands they controlled

comedy A humorous play

democracy A form of government in which leaders are chosen by citizens who vote

diplomat A person who represents a country, usually when communicating with or visiting other countries

discus A heavy disc; also a sport in which a discus is thrown

dowry Money or goods given to a woman's husband before their marriage

epics Long poems that usually celebrate a country's heroes and history

fertile Able to produce lots of crops

fleets Groups of ships that sail together

flourished Achieved great success

frieze A narrow band of sculpture around the top of a building

heroes Adventurers who show great bravery and courage, and who are often remembered in stories

hoplite A heavily-armed foot soldier

interpret To figure out the meaning

irrigate To carry water to crops, usually through a system of human-made channels

javelin A long spear; also a sport in which the javelin is thrown

marble A hard-wearing stone used for buildings and statues

merchants People who buy and sell goods

myths Well-known stories which have been told for generations

nutrients Substances living things need to grow

oligarchy A form of government in which power is held by a few people

patron A god or goddess who protects something specific, such as harvests

philosopher A person who studies ideas, such as the meaning of life, in search of truth and understanding

politics The way a government works; how its ideas are put into practice

proverb A well-known saying that states the truth or gives advice

punches Metal tools used to make patterns or holes

reason Using logic to form judgments

replica An exact copy

sacrificed Killed to please the gods

temples Buildings where gods are worshiped

terra-cotta A reddish-brown clay that is hardened by baking

tragedy A serious or sad play

trial by jury A system of asking a group of people to decide if a person is guilty of a crime

Trojans Inhabitants of the city of Troy, in modern-day Turkey

widowed When a woman's husband has died

Learning More

Want to learn more about ancient Greece? Check out these resources.

Books

Covert, Kim. *Ancient Greece: Birthplace of Democracy*. Capstone Press, 2012.

Dickmann, Nancy. *Ancient Greece*. Capstone Press, 2016.

Hyde, Natalie. *Understanding Greek Myths*. Crabtree Publishing, 2012.

Pearson, Anne. *Ancient Greece*. DK Children, 2014.

Waldron, Melanie. *Geography Matters in Ancient Greece*. Heinemann-Raintree, 2015.

Wood, Alix. *Uncovering the Culture of Ancient Greece*. Rosen Publishing, 2016.

Websites

Learn more about the process of ostracism through artifacts and primary-source texts from the American School of Classical Studies at Athens.
www.agathe.gr/democracy/practice_of_ostracism.html

Explore ancient Greece in this comprehensive site from the British Museum.
www.ancientgreece.co.uk

The Canadian Museum of History website covers many topics about ancient Greece, and includes a timeline and activities.
www.historymuseum.ca/cmc/exhibitions/civil/greece/gr1010e.shtml

Explore an interactive map that follows the journey of Odysseus, the hero of Homer's epics *The Iliad* and *The Odyssey*. The site includes additional links to more information about ancient Greek mythology.
http://0nationalgeographic.org/maps/travels-odysseus

Learn all about the ancient Olympic Games on this site presented by the International Olympic Committee.
www.olympic.org/ancient-olympic-games

Smart History presents an informative video on Athens as the birthplace of democracy that includes information about important sites in the ancient city.
http://smarthistory.org/the-athenian-agora-and-the-experiment-in-democracy

INDEX

ABOUT THE AUTHOR

John Malam studied Ancient History and Archaeology at the University of Birmingham, England. He has written many information books for children, particularly on ancient civilizations.